Divorce

Overcome The Overwhelm and Avoid
The Six Biggest Mistakes—Insights From
Personal Divorce Coaches

PRAISE FOR

*Divorce: Overcome the Overwhelm and
Avoid the Six Biggest Mistakes—Insights From
Personal Divorce Coaches*

"I absolutely love what Pegotty and Randall Cooper have to say in this book.

I have done so much research and writing on issues pertaining to lawyer limitations, particularly when it comes to matters involving families. Lawyers serve a necessary and useful purpose in family law matters and for society as a whole. For one thing, they warn of unforeseen 'what- ifs.' Furthermore, words have meaning and the difference between 'may' and 'shall' could substantially change the meaning of a provision. Lawyers are wordsmiths in that regard. Moreover, divorce is a legal process.

Through working with qualified personal Divorce Coaches and other such professionals, lawyers' limitations can be overcome. In putting together the right 'team,' divorcing couples can obtain better results at a lower overall cost. In this book, the Coopers help to explain how the 'game of divorce' should be designed to improve the odds of a successful outcome in the grand scheme of life."

—Mark B. Baer, Esq.
Family Law Attorney/Mediator/Collaborative Law Practitioner

"This book offers a step-by-step process to confront divorce and take the necessary actions for a healthy divorce. Use this book and you will reduce the amount of time, money and emotion you expend on your divorce by no less than fifty percent. The questions at the end of each chapter offer many insights. This book can be used as a vehicle when going through divorce and also as a reflection and completion of anything unresolved as a result of the divorce. Bravo."

—Debbie Schwarz
Judicial Assistant
Family Court Division of State of Florida

"This workbook will help you take charge of your divorce and ensure that you avoid the six most common mistakes. The authors provide easy-to-use problem solving tools and thoughtful exercises to help you rein in the emotions surrounding your divorce, and plan for the business side of the process. I applaud Pegotty and Randy for developing this workbook to help people during each stage of their divorce."

—Laura Woodard
President, GrassRoots Marketing Group, Inc.

"Pegotty and Randy Cooper provide a practical set of tools readers can use to assess exactly where they are in the divorce process, where they want to wind up, and how to get there in an efficient, empowered and ethical manner."

—David C. Barry, J.D., L.S.W.
Certified Divorce Coach® and Mediator

"Pegotty and Randall encourage readers to embrace their feelings and be their best selves in the face of divorce. Using this book and the process provided by these trusted coaches will help you maintain your power and dignity as you navigate the overwhelm of divorce."

—Carla Higgins
Divorced mother of three young daughters

"As a person who's gone through the divorce process, I understand the pain, overwhelm, confusion, and guilt that accompany the break-up of a family. Seeking guidance of trained professionals to facilitate healing is important, and Pegotty and Randall provide healthy and positive support in this book. Each chapter provides an overview of a mistake, insights about each problem, and then helps you develop clarity and a course of action before taking your next steps. The workbook format is especially helpful because it offers an opportunity for you to learn and grow as you reflect and write.

People make many mistakes during divorce, and Pegotty and Randall effectively focus on the most important ones to avoid, and then help you adopt new perspectives for a healthier divorce and a happier future. I recommend this book for anyone who feels overwhelmed by divorce."

—Kim Clausen
Denver, CO

"A much-needed gem! Laid out in an easy-to-follow format—that takes much of the hassle out of sorting through the inevitable 'gunk' of a divorce—this book will evolutionize how people experience and successfully navigate all the potential traps and pitfalls of their divorce. The authors help you confidently put your divorce in the very best hands—YOURS!"

—Laurie Cameron
Master Certified Relationship Coach, Mentor Coach
Author of *The Journey from Fear to Love*

"Divorce can be the biggest emotional upheaval we face in a lifetime. This book reminds us to think about long-term personal goals and consider what we want to accomplish *after* our divorce so we can stay focused on these goals *during* our divorce."

—Sue Lehman
Oakland, CA

"When I read a preview copy of this book, I found myself wishing I'd had access to this information—and a personal Divorce Coach—when I experienced divorce many years ago. A personal Divorce Coach would have encouraged me to carefully examine my choices, and perhaps I would never have given up the alimony and child support I needed and deserved. Because I was emotionally drained, I listened to my attorney, and now I realize he wasn't working in my best interest. It's all water under a long ago bridge, but it was a costly experience.

For those who are facing divorce today, this book is a good start to coaching yourself and finding your own wisdom. Pegotty and Randall bring their extensive experience and genuine hearts to this topic. I recommend their work and this book without reservation."

—Lorraine Lane
Business Coach and Author of *Business-Building Referrals*
www.lorrainelane.com

"The authors of this book, personal Divorce Coaches, provide you with perspective on what to do—and what not to do—when navigating the journey of divorce. They offer you a roadmap with hazard warnings to keep you on track."

—Wendy Ellen Coughlin, Ph.D.
Licensed Mental Health Counselor
Supreme Court of Florida Certified Family Mediator
and Parenting Coordinator

Divorce Coaching, Inc.
8729 Bay Pointe Dr.
Tampa, FL 33615

www.CertifiedDivorceCoach.com

ISBN: 978-0-9915314-0-0

Printed in the United States of America
First Printing 2014

Limits of Liability/Disclaimer: The authors and/or publisher do not guarantee that anyone following the techniques, suggestions, tips, ideas, or strategies in this book will have success. The reader assumes all responsibility and liability for the use of the information contained herein. The author and/or publisher shall have neither liability nor responsibility to anyone with respect to any loss or damage caused, or alleged to be caused, directly or indirectly by the information contained in this book. This book is not a substitute for professional counseling.

Cover design by
Toten Creative

Interior artwork by
Kara Brown

Interior design by
Nand Kishore Pandey

To all those going through divorce, this book is our gift to you.
If we help just one person avoid one of the biggest mistakes,
it will have been worth it to us to write this book.
Unwrap your gift.

Pegotty and Randall R. Cooper

Divorce

Overcome The Overwhelm and Avoid
The Six Biggest Mistakes—Insights From
Personal Divorce Coaches

Pegotty Cooper
and
Randall R. Cooper

CONTENTS

THE OVERWHELMING
NATURE OF DIVORCE

Divorce. It's a word that certainly didn't enter your mind on the day you said, "I do." Never in a million years did you think you'd be facing divorce—but here you are. It's now a very real part of your life.

According to the American Institute of Stress, divorce is one of the most stressful processes a person can undergo, second only to the death of a spouse.[1] In fact, many people equate divorce with the death of a marriage. Coming to terms with the fact that you and your spouse will not experience *till death do us* part can exact emotional and physical tolls—and overwhelm every aspect of your life.

Between the difficulties of explaining the end of the marriage to family and friends, the grief over the loss of a valued relationship, and the pressure and anxiety of dealing with a legal process that has its own protocols and language it's easy for those going through divorce to become overwhelmed to the point where they are out of touch with their everyday lives and have difficulty executing what used to be a normal routine. Your work life may be affected, your social life may change, and your emotional and physical health may suffer.

Work Life

Peak performance at work becomes challenging during divorce. Your feelings of failure in your marriage may transfer to your work. You

---

[1] Source: www.stress.org

may begin to view your work as insignificant or regard your work in a negative way, which could lead to subpar performance. You may also be distracted and unable to focus on the quality of your work and the attainment of your goals. This puts your future at risk at a time when you definitely do not need additional overwhelming stressors.

Social Life

You may find being around others is overwhelming during divorce, so you begin to detach from friends and family. Loneliness and depression can overcome you, and many times you may respond in unintentionally crass or crude ways because you feel so over-powered. You know you're not acting like the "real you," but you can't help yourself—and others may no longer be willing or able to approach you.

Those you may be counting on to be part of your support circle may also feel their loyalty is torn and, rather than choosing allegiance to either "side," your friends may back away to avoid being perceived as favoring one particular person or the other.

Family Life

Whether you realize it or not, when you're overwhelmed by divorce you may isolate yourself from family members or pick unnecessary fights out of jealousy for a real or imagined situation. If children are involved, divorce can also overwhelm parenting. At a time when parental awareness is critical, you may be unable to focus on the day-to-day attention your children so badly need.
Physical and Mental Health

Lack of sleep, poor eating habits, emotional turmoil, and loss of exercise all contribute to feeling deluged and overwhelmed during divorce. When you don't feel your best physically and men-tally, dealing with even the slightest challenge is difficult, and di-vorce usually involves tremendous stress and major upheavals that require huge reserves of physical and emotional strength and resil-ience ("bounce-back-ability").

Everyday Life

The overwhelming nature of divorce can challenge your cognitive abilities and influence even your simplest thoughts and actions. What you usually consider to be routine tasks and easy decisions suddenly take monumental efforts to achieve. Simple things such as obeying a stoplight, picking up the dry cleaning, ensuring the security system for the home has been activated or simply taking out the trash on time become a challenge. When you're overwhelmed, you experience a decline in thinking skills, the ability to remember and reason, and the ability to make sound decisions.

Divorce is a process that can overwhelm your life. If not approached properly, decisions made during this period can result in serious mistakes that can have long-term consequences for everyone involved. The overwhelming nature of divorce leads to six common, yet entirely avoidable, mistakes: forgetting who the decision makers are, taking a "my way or the highway" approach to negotiation, limiting your resources to only your attorney, throwing in the towel, betting the farm on another relationship, and wanting guarantees and certainty. These six mistakes are far from inconsequential mishaps: They can lead to a number of major legal, financial, and other wrong turns.

So, how do you cope with being overwhelmed and avoid the six biggest mistakes people make in divorce? How can you embark on your journey, maintain your dignity and sense of self, and make the best decisions? The first step is to acknowledge that, while divorce can be overwhelming, any obstacles the process presents can be overcome *with the help of others*. Now is not the time to try to "go it alone." There are too many important decisions to make, and you need personal and professional support as you travel through the mounds of legal, financial and emotional issues you face. Certain experts can explain the legalities, outline your options, and identify the consequences, but not all professionals can *help you help yourself.*

That's what a *personal Divorce Coach* does. A personal Divorce Coach provides guidance as you sort through your thoughts, helps you tap into your creative and problem-solving skills, and prepares you mentally for the rollercoaster of emotions you'll experience. A Divorce Coach ensures you don't have to "go it alone."

In this book we are giving you insights about how to coach yourself as a start to moving through the overwhelm which often leads to making the biggest avoidable mistakes in divorce. Use the insights we have gotten from our work with hundreds of divorce clients to help you tap into your wisdom. And if after doing the reflective exercises in this book you aren't getting the traction you want, or you keep finding yourself in the overwhelm, a personal Divorce Coach can be a great partner in helping you to move forward, to gain clarity and confidence so that you have the courage to move forward in your divorce journey.

PERSONAL DIVORCE COACHES

Whenever we hear the term *coach* in connection with football, baseball, or any other sport, we automatically understand what a coach is and what a coach does: coaches support their teams by providing strategy, tactics, and feedback to achieve the overall goal of winning. In recent years, particularly in the last decade, industries other than sports have embraced the coaching concept. Personal coaching has emerged as a significant force in helping people overcome the obstacles which prevent them from moving forward. Personal coaching does not replace therapy or mental health counseling; and many professionals have begun to develop a parallel practice of coaching as part of their service to clients.

The International Coach Federation, recognized widely for establishing the core competencies of coaching, defines coaching as "partnering with clients in a thought-provoking and creative process that inspires them to maximize their personal and professional potential. It is an ongoing professional relationship that helps people produce extraordinary results in their lives, careers, businesses, or organizations." In other words, not unlike sports coaches, personal coaches work together with their clients to assess where they are today and help them set goals for where they want to be in the future. Coaches then help their clients create and execute the plans to achieve those goals. Personal Divorce Coaches do that as well, and they specialize in helping those going through divorce. Personal Divorce Coaches may be called upon during any of the three phases of divorce.

The Three Phases of Divorce

The divorce process encompasses three phases: pre-, during, and post- divorce. The pre-divorce phase begins the moment you first experience frustration, insecurity, or dissatisfaction in your marriage and consider divorcing a viable option. During this phase, you may suspect things aren't right and fear finding out the truth. You may also have a gut feeling your spouse has already abandoned the relationship. It's not uncommon for many individuals to develop deep issues of anxiety and anger that can take an emotional and physical toll.

You may ask yourself: *Should I or shouldn't I? What should I be doing now to protect myself? How can I ensure stability for my family? What plans do I need to make if, indeed, divorce is the answer?*

The second phase of divorce, during divorce, can be a tumultuous process for both spouses as they enter this period of transition from married to legally-divorced. This stage usually begins with one spouse's decision to dissolve the marriage and ends with the legal settlement and divorce decree.

Once the legal process is complete, the post-divorce phase begins. Now that all assets have been divided, and the divorce is final, you can take positive steps and move toward the next chapter in your life.

How Can a Personal Divorce Coach Help?

When anyone undergoes a life-changing experience, it's important to have as many support systems in place as possible. Although family and friends may give sympathy and encouragement, they can't provide the expert advice and support of a personal Divorce Coach.

Sound Decision Making

A personal Divorce Coach provides you with a sounding board and thinking partner, a professional who can help you make *sound* decisions based on rational choices and practicalities rather than on sheer emotion and impulsive behavior. Sound decision making entails looking at various options and assessing how each will likely unfold in the future. It also involves being willing to listen to others whose opinion may differ from your own, as well as seeking the perspectives of experts who have a better view of how these situations like yours usually turn out in a court of law and in real life. And, let's face reality: Divorce is a highly emotional process for almost everyone involved. A personal Divorce Coach will help you step back from your immediate emotions and understand what you to believe to be your best-case and worst-case scenarios, and that will help you in discussions with your attorney or mediator.

Goal Setting

A personal Divorce Coach works with you to set and achieve goals—for yourself and your family. This includes taking the next step in preparing yourself for the process of divorce, as well as laying the foundations for a successful future and helping you transition to your new role as you enter the next chapter of your life.

Building Resilience

Resilience is an individual's ability to bounce back from tough times. A process for pulling out the strengths you already have and enhancing your ability to find the reserves to keep going in a more-than-difficult situation. A personal Divorce Coach helps you build your personal strategy for resilience so you can deal more effectively with the change and disappointment of divorce.

Remaining True to Your Purpose and Values

When you are overwhelmed by divorce, you may cast aside your personal values or standards, and forget about your life purpose. A personal Divorce Coach will help you reacquaint yourself with your values and determine which of those values you want to fully honor during the divorce process. (For a complimentary values assessment, please visit www.CertifiedDivorceCoach.com/values.) If you've never given thought to your life purpose, there is no better time than the present. Don't worry if it sounds cumbersome: Your personal Divorce Coach will guide you through this process.

Tim Kelley, in his book, *True Purpose* [2], defines life purpose as "the difference you're meant to make." Keeping your personal values and "the difference you're meant to make" front and center during your divorce will make your decisions easier and your choices more clear.

Leaving Your Baggage at the Door

We all have "baggage" we carry around with us: judgments, thoughts, feelings, automatic ways of responding, past experiences, and more that affect our behavior and decisions. As you enter the divorce process, it's important to let go of that baggage—or at least leave it at the door. You don't need additional worries overshadowing your interactions with your children, spouse or the divorce professionals with whom you'll work throughout your journey. Your personal Divorce Coach helps you examine your baggage and figure out how to put it aside until you're ready to get rid of it completely.

Alternative Approaches

A personal Divorce Coach can help you understand the various process options available to you as you navigate the process of divorce. The most common methods, depending upon the circumstances, include retaining separate family attorneys to represent each spouse, engaging in collaborative divorce, joining together to hire a mediator, or engaging in self-representation.

Personal Divorce Coaches work with you in a very holistic way and help you to address a wide variety of concerns that come up during the divorce process. Their multifaceted approach includes helping you examine your particular needs and helping you understand the impact

---

[2] *True Purpose* by Tim Kelley. Transcendent Solutions Press (April 1, 2009)

of every decision you make from start to finish. A personal Divorce Coach can help you through the rough spots in your divorce in three areas: the business of divorce; setting and accomplishing goals, and doing the internal work that leads to a happier and healthier life. Personal Divorce Coaches help you in ways that include understanding the impact of the decision to divorce and getting organized for the process to helping you communicate more effectively. In short, they'll help you avoid the biggest mistakes people make in divorce. When you can nip these mistakes in the bud it is easier to change the course of your divorce.

Your personal Divorce Coach will provide an understanding, nonjudgmental, and patient environment that nurtures you as an individual and fosters feelings of safety and support. This environment, which coaches are specifically trained in, helps empower clients. And because personal Divorce Coaches don't dispense legal advice, they're not bound to serving clients by geographical limitations.

A personal Divorce Coach:

- prepares you for the process of divorce by helping you organize papers and other materials, recording questions you may have, and providing a sounding board as you clarify your priorities about property, parenting, and future needs.

- helps you avoid huge emotional and financial mistakes.
- identifies key areas of decision-making during the divorce process.
- helps you employ a sound decision-making process.
- focuses on what's important to you and helps you set goals accordingly.
- works with you to define a path for achieving your goals, and supports you as you move forward.
- helps you to build a strategy for building resilience and using your best strengths.
- enhances your understanding of the divorce process by providing professional experience and educational resources.
- helps you develop better communication skills so you will be more credible during the legal process.
- helps you understand the potential pitfalls you may encounter and provides you with strategies for avoiding these pitfalls.
- assists you with resources during the divorce transition and helps you lay new foundations for the future.

ABOUT THE AUTHORS

Pegotty Cooper and Randall R. Cooper have been happily married for 30 years. Both of their first marriages ended in divorce. Today, they are not only partners in marriage, they also are partners in business: They are the founders of Divorce Coaching, Inc., a firm that trains and certifies individuals to become personal Divorce Coaches.

After 25 years working in executive positions in large organizations, Pegotty decided to start her own coaching practice. She's been coaching—and assisting people undergoing divorce—for more than a decade. In addition to her experience in life and business, Pegotty's qualifications include certifications from several highly reputable coach training organizations: the Coach Training Alliance, 6 Advisors Coaching Academy, Arbinger Institute, ReCareer Institute, and The Productive Tension Institute.

Randall enjoyed a long career in the Financial Services industry, including executive positions at major financial institutions, and ultimately established his own fee-only financial planning practice. After becoming a Certified Divorce Financial Analyst™, in 2005 Randall was certified as a family mediator by the Supreme Court of Florida.

As a family mediator, he facilitates negotiations between couples during all aspects of the decision-making process and helps them reach a settlement agreement.

After he was certified as a Financial Coach in 2010, Randall experienced a revelation: Although he enjoyed working as a family mediator, he really wanted to also work with *individuals* involved in the divorce process. Because mediators are not permitted to work with only one spouse, Randall decided he also wanted to be a personal Divorce Coach. At that time, most personal Divorce Coaches focused on the post-divorce transition of their clients. Randall, however, knew that the greatest opportunity to make a difference in the outcomes of the divorce process occurs at the beginning of the process: helping each client view the overall process, determine clear wants and needs, and plan short- and long-term strategies to effectively maneuver through the divorce process while avoiding the biggest, most common mistakes people make.

Randall's original idea has since gained momentum, and three years ago, he and Pegotty founded Divorce Coaching, Inc. To develop a curriculum that would meet the high standards for their CDC Certified Divorce Coach® training and certification program—taught through the CDC College for Divorce Coaching®—Randall and Pegotty consulted several highly trained and experienced professionals who serve individuals engaged in the divorce process. CDC Certified Divorce Coaches must meet rigorous standards established by the CDC Board of Standards®. To date, Pegotty and Randall have graduated more than 50 personal Divorce Coaches and have conducted dozens of classes on *The Biggest Mistakes People Make in Divorce*.

Pegotty and Randall developed the CDC College for Divorce Coaching®, the CDC Board of Standards®, Divorce Coach Ethics and Professional Responsibilities guidelines, and additional requirements to establish professional criteria for Divorce Coaching.

Pegotty and Randall reside in the Tampa Bay area with their two adopted cats, and enjoy all of the activities and natural attractions on the west coast of Florida: walking on the beach, snorkeling, birding, kayaking, biking, and exploring.

HOW TO USE THIS WORKBOOK

The first six chapters examine the biggest mistakes people make when going through divorce. The beginning of each of these chapters is comprised of three sections: an overview of the mistake, the potential consequences of the mistake, and insights from personal Divorce Coaches. Read these first three sections of each chapter a few times until you fully understand them.

Next, it's time for some reflection on your part. The "Develop Clarity and Take Action" sections are comprised of five segments, each with reflective questions and space to write your answers:

1. Walk Down the Path

When you walk down the path, you'll explore your journey with open mindedness and curiosity, enabling you to envision the likely outcome of your current course. By doing so, you will avoid feeling overwhelmed and making a particular misstep. You will identify the resources you have to support your decisions and other options you could consider.

2. Seek Expert Perspective

As you go through your divorce, many experts are available who can address your needs including family attorneys, tax planners, family mediators, certified divorce financial analysts, psychotherapists, parenting professionals, and property appraisers, etc. Seeking the view of such experts can help alleviate your stress and lessen your feelings of being overwhelmed.

In this section of each chapter, you'll focus on determining what additional information you may need, and obtaining input from professionals who can support you.

3. Expand Your Capacity

Learning new strategies, expanding your reserves, and developing new skills and habits will increase your problem-solving skills. In "Expanding Your Capacity," you will contemplate ways to think outside of the box, develop a new perspective, and create options to better serve your goals.

4. Align with Your Best Self

Maintaining your equilibrium and facing challenging decisions with grace and dignity enhances your confidence and decision-making abilities. In this section, you will reflect on your thoughts, feelings, and behaviors and concentrate on how to remain true to yourself, your values, and your purpose.

5. Your Next Step

The divorce process is not a cakewalk, and you'll need to muster all the resilience and determination you can to take decisive action, demonstrate grace under fire, and continue to move forward. In this section, you'll determine one small step you can take to move forward and avoid this particular mistake.

This process of developing clarity and taking action can also be used by you in other situations where you might find yourself overwhelmed.

Should you wish to hire a personal Divorce Coach, Chapter Seven will provide you with insight and guidelines to help you find the right professional for you.

Finally, at the end of this workbook, there is a Resources section that provides you with a reading list and links to websites you may want to explore further.

Chapter 1

MISTAKE ONE:
FORGETTING WHO THE DECISION
MAKERS ARE

I hired a lawyer right away. That's what everyone else does. He's an experienced divorce attorney, and I trust him. There are so many decisions to make, and I think he's got a good grasp on my situation. He'll make the best decisions for me and my family.

It's only natural to feel bombarded by choices during the divorce process, but it's never good to assume your lawyer automatically knows what's best for you. While it seems much easier to let someone else (your attorney) deal with all the details and make all the decisions, you may be assuming he has more insight into your needs than he actually has. Giving him the freedom to act on your behalf without consulting you can result in huge mistakes.

Those going through divorce often believe the decision makers are the attorneys and the judge. Your attorney is not the decision maker: The decision makers in divorce are you and your spouse.

Don't assume your lawyer has super powers. Just because he's a skilled divorce lawyer doesn't necessarily mean he's an expert in business, finance, real estate, taxes, insurance, etc. You may think you'll expedite the process and save money and time by having your divorce attorney serve in more than one capacity, but you might end up losing more than you'll save in the long run.

Consequences of Forgetting Who the Decision Makers Are

By placing all decision making in the hands of your lawyer—either because your lawyer takes on that role, or because you don't want to make the decisions—you're relinquishing control of your own future. Abdicating decision making to someone else—whether it's your lawyer, spouse or a (hopefully) sympathetic judge—can have negative, and sometimes irreversible, consequences.

If you and your spouse cannot make the necessary decisions, the only other person who can is the judge. Please don't think that once you have your day in court and the judge hears the whole truth, she'll mete out her own form of "emotional" justice to that irresponsible, selfish person you were married to for all those years. It's a nice dream, but don't count on it. Although most people expect a judge to be the final decision maker, in reality, more than 90 percent of all cases settle before the final hearing or trial. The other cases settle outside of court with the assistance of lawyers and other professionals, including a personal Divorce Coach. When a divorce does go to court, the judge makes decisions based not on what is important to you, but on the legally relevant and admissible facts of the case, among other things, and their own interpretations.

Insights from Personal Divorce Coaches

1. During the divorce process you have the right to self-determination. In other words, both you and your spouse retain the power to make your own decisions. If you cannot agree on certain points, your attorney can advise you, but cannot

dictate your decisions. If, however, the dispute should end up in court, the judge will decide.

2. Because attorneys have legal expertise and knowledge of what is customary, they're usually well equipped to advise you. But in all cases, you are the decision maker, and ultimately, you're the one who must agree to the terms of the marital settlement. As the decision maker, you have the right to accept your attorney's advice or explore other options to ensure you make the best decisions for yourself.

3. You may be pressured during the process to expedite your decisions in order to meet certain deadlines. If you feel rushed, your attorney may be able to negotiate for more time.

The Key Idea:

Retain your right to make decisions; don't abdicate to others. Do consider their advice while weighing all options.

Develop Clarity and Take Action

1. Walk down the Path

There is no such thing as *emotional* justice in the courtroom. If your case comes before a judge, *legal* justice will determine the outcome. You may not think it's fair, but that's how the legal system works.

What actions do you need to take to ensure you retain control of your own decision making during the divorce process?

_____

_____

_____

If you've turned over the decision making to your attorney or your spouse, what do you need to do now to take back decision making?

_____

_____

_____

2. Seek Expert Perspective

What additional information do you feel you need in order to retain control over your decisions?

_____

_____

_____

What expert perspectives might be helpful in your decision making?

_____

_____

_____

Where can you find these resources?

_____

_____

_____

3. Expand Your Capacity

You can expand your decision-making capacity by developing greater clarity about the options available to you. Think about a decision you are considering and describe 2-3 additional options available.

_____

_____

_____

What can you do to ensure that you maintain a healthy, clear mind throughout the decision-making process without relinquishing control to others?

_____

_____

_____

4. Align with Your Best Self

People often react to emotional situations in uncharacteristic ways and then regret their choices. When you clarify your purpose and remain true to your personal values, you'll find decision making less difficult.

How do you want yourself and others, including your children, to remember your actions during the divorce process?

_____

_____

_____

When you assess your overall approach during this difficult time, what one-word term do you hope describes you?

_____

_____

_____

Which of your personal values do you want to be certain to honor during your divorce?

_____

_____

_____

We experience many negative emotions during divorce, including grief, anger, and loss. What are you most thankful for, despite any negative feelings?

_____

_____

_____

5. Your Next Step

What small step can you take to move forward to ensure you consider all options and do not abdicate your decision making?

_____

_____

_____

On a scale of 1-10, how important is this step to you? _____

What will be accomplished when you take this step?

_____

_____

_____

By when will you take this step?

_____

_____

_____

Whom will you ask for support?

_____

_____

_____

How Can a Personal Divorce Coach Help?

A personal Divorce Coach…

- explores with you who and how you want to be throughout your divorce, and helps you determine what is most important to you.
- helps ensure your commitment to yourself so you don't get hijacked as a result of aggressive behavior on the part of your spouse or attorney.
- identifies key areas of decision making during the divorce process, and ensures you maintain control over your decisions.
- works with you to clarify your purpose and remain true to your values, rendering decision making less difficult.
- helps you explore more options and refers you to other experts.

> *"We gain strength, and courage, and confidence by each experience in which we really stop to look fear in the face. We must do that which we think we cannot."*

—Eleanor Roosevelt

Chapter 2

MISTAKE TWO:
"MY WAY OR THE HIGHWAY"
STYLE OF NEGOTIATION

I try to tell my spouse I know what's best, but he refuses to listen. He just says, "No," with no explanation, folds his arms, and refuses to talk. He won't even discuss my solution. When we meet, it just ends up in a shouting match, and then he gives me the silent treatment.

She accuses me of digging in my heels and being obstinate—says I refuse to listen to her views. And when I say, "OK, let's talk," she doesn't show up at hearings. She and her attorney still won't deliver the information my attorney has asked for.

Even though you're spending lots of money to do so, you choose to challenge your spouse on almost every issue because you want to win at all costs. The desire to win is natural, but engaging in an adversarial divorce—by hoping to wear down your spouse and achieve the ultimate victory—may end up being more time consuming, emotionally draining, and costly than you realize. In fact, the only one who may benefit from your stubbornness is your lawyer, who has gained a long-term client.

If you have children and refuse to listen to any of your spouse's views, you're not considering the impact your actions may have on your children. Because you refuse to budge and continue to approach decisions with a "my way or the highway" attitude, you're focused only on getting your own way, and often ignore what's most important: your children's wellbeing, including their financial support, custodial concerns, and future relationship with you.

Consequences of Taking the "My Way or the Highway" Style of Negotiation

The "I win, you lose" approach rarely results in a workable solution. When either spouse or both spouses stand their ground and refuse to cooperate, it's ultimately a "no win" situation. The "my way or the highway" stance can lead to higher legal costs, a longer divorce process, and increased negativity in the form of court surprises or more legal motions. Relationships may be damaged, good solutions may be ignored, and in the end, your obstinacy causes more stress, tension, and anger—and leaves you feeling overwhelmed.

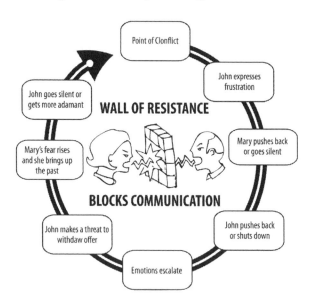

Using this approach often leads to a vicious tug-of-war as each spouse tries to outdo the other. Clients sometimes spend tens of thousands in legal fees defending their right to be right, but that doesn't guarantee them an ironclad "victory." *In fact, the more you dig in your heels and insist you're right, the less likely it is that a reasonable agreement will be reached.*

Maintaining effective communications during the divorce process is challenging when emotions overcome logic. It's human nature: the harder one person pushes, the more the other person resists. However, with the "my way or the highway" approach, more energy is wasted on the fight than invested in finding a solution.

Insights from Personal Divorce Coaches

1. "My way or the highway" creates barriers to communication. If you indicate you're willing to listen to what your spouse is saying, then your spouse may be willing to listen to you. All human beings want to be heard and understood and, regardless of gender or age, most will become defensive when they're being ignored or unfairly judged.

2. Conversely, people open themselves up to new ideas when they believe the other person "gets" how they feel. Hang up the boxing gloves, listen without interruption, try to understand what is important to the other person, and hear what they are really saying. Through your actions, let that person know you respect their right to convey their point of view, and that you have listened to what they've said

3. Be clear about what's most important to you and ask for it. The more credible you are, the more say you have in the final results.

4. Keep your hot buttons in check and let go of the past.

The Key Idea:

Listen for what's important to your spouse and allow give and take to reach agreement.

Develop Clarity and Take Action

 ### 1. Walk down the Path

The "my way or the highway" approach often results in a wall of resistance that completely blocks communication.

What issue often causes conflict between you and your spouse?

_____

_____

_____

How does your spouse push your hot buttons?

_____

_____

_____

How do you feel when that happens?

_____

_____

_____

How do you react?

_____

_____

_____

How does your spouse respond to your reaction?

_____

_____

_____

How does their response make you feel?

_____

_____

_____

What is *your* response to *their* reaction?

_____

_____

_____

How will this conversation end?

_____

_____

_____

What is the likely result?

_____

_____

_____

Will this result cause you to lose more of your resources (time, money, and other resources-)?

_____

_____

_____

2. Seek Expert Perspective

What kind of help do you need to avoid taking the "my way or the highway" stance?

_____

_____

_____

What type of assistance do you need to facilitate your interaction with a spouse who makes communication difficult?

_____

_____

_____

Where will you find these resources?

_____

_____

_____

3. Expand Your Capacity

If you are experiencing resistance from your spouse, let go of your past feelings of hurt and anger, and step into their world to hear what they are saying.

What "baggage" might you be carrying around with you that could impact this interaction?

_____

_____

_____

Reflect on a time when you may not have been willing to hear what your spouse is saying. Briefly describe this instance.

_____

_____

_____

What impact does your unwillingness to listen have on him or her?

_____

_____

_____

What common ground might you find with your spouse that could lead to more productive communication?

_____

_____

_____

4. Align with Your Best Self

Your reactions to your spouse during the divorce process can create conflict or cooperation.

How are you showing up in conversations and negotiations?

_____

_____

_____

What efforts are you making to be respected and heard?

_____

_____

_____

What efforts are you making to respect and hear the other person?

_____

_____

_____

What changes might you make so your conversations line up with what is most important for you and remain consistent with your values?

_____

_____

_____

5. Your Next Step

What small step can you take to move forward and establish open communication that allows for give and take in your negotiations?

_____

_____

_____

On a scale of 1-10, how important is this step to you? _____

What will be accomplished when you take this step?

_____

_____

_____

By when will you take this step?

_____

_____

_____

Whom will you ask for support?

_____

_____

_____

How Can a Personal Divorce Coach Help?

A personal Divorce Coach…

- helps you clarify your wants and needs.
- helps you gain perspective and develop a healthy approach for keeping the lines of communication open with your spouse, your lawyer, your family, and your support team.
- works with you to determine the best way to ask for what you want and need.
- prepares you for potential interactions, through role play activities and other means, so you feel comfortable when presenting your wants and needs to your spouse.

> *"Choosing to be positive and having a grateful attitude is going to determine how you're going to live your life."*
>
> —Joel Osteen

Chapter 3

MISTAKE THREE:
LIMITING YOUR RESOURCES

I just got served papers for divorce, and I don't know where to turn for help. I think I'll ask my friends for the name of a divorce attorney, and I guess he'll just handle everything for me. Or maybe I'll handle it all myself. That way, it'll be cheaper, and I can use the money I save to live on in the future.

As you go through the divorce process, you'll be required to make many decisions that will affect your future. Given that a full 50 percent of marriages end in divorce, it's likely you have a friend or family member who has been through a divorce, so you have a feel for what you should do: get advice from friends and/or family members who have been through the divorce process, and hire an attorney to handle everything. Yes, you need to consult a competent and caring family attorney because the divorce process involves legal issues, but you may be limiting your ability to resolve every issue satisfactorily if you rely solely on the perspective of one professional. It's not fair—to you or to your attorney— to expect him or her to know everything and handle everything.

Aside from legal procedures, other facets of divorce require special consideration. These can include decisions about finances, business, parenting, career, special issues, etc. The details involved can be very complex, and seeking assistance from experienced experts will bring a fresh perspective and enhance your decision-making abilities.

Like it or not, the divorce process often forces you to make some of the most critical personal and business decisions you'll ever make—decisions that can impact the rest of your life. Is it really prudent to take these steps without expert advisors and guides who respect your views and honor your needs?

Consequences of Limiting Your Resources

During divorce, many people are so overwhelmed with stress and other negative emotions that they lose their ability to reason effectively by as much as 30 percent. Often, when this happens, people don't realize that their abilities to process and make clear-headed decisions have been hindered, and you may ultimately pay the price: there may be tax and financial errors of which you are not aware. (Yes, this happens.) There is also the possibility of future legal fees for returning to court for items that were overlooked.

Whenever we're overwhelmed, our judgment is affected. Regardless of whether you think you know how to handle a situation or are wracked with indecision, you may want to seek other expert perspectives to validate your assumptions or guide you to a logical decision. Each divorce involves a unique set of circumstances and requires specific choices, and every decision you make impacts your future. Your lawyer can handle the legal dissolution of your marriage but to avoid post-divorce problems in other areas that can result in additional legal fees, the expertise of professionals in addition to your attorney might be beneficial.

Insights from Personal Divorce Coaches

1. Keep a notebook and calendar with you at all times. Use the notebook to record any questions or thoughts that pop

into your mind. Identify deadlines (such as court deadlines and filing requirements) and record them on your calendar. Use a page in your notebook to record these deadlines and next to each deadline, record the details of what needs to be done.

2. Use a page in your notebook just for questions. Make three columns: In the first column, write your question. In the next column, indicate what type of question it is (legal, financial, child-related, etc.). In the third column, indicate where you might get your answer. You may want to leave a space under the question to write in the answer.

3. Most professionals offer an initial consultation to determine if they are the right resource for you and fit your situation. Providing a list of questions for these professionals will help them answer that question and make the best use of both your time and theirs.

> ### The Key Idea:
> It's not reasonable to think that one resource (like your attorney) can know everything; look for insight and support from a variety of experienced resources.

Develop Clarity and Take Action

1. Walk down the Path

The decisions you make during your divorce will affect you for the rest of your life.

What steps in your decision-making process may present obstacles or blind spots that may prevent you from seeing the whole picture? (It may be difficult to answer this question, but consider decisions you're so confident about that you haven't bothered to verify your assumptions.)

_____

_____

_____

What happens if your current assumptions are totally incorrect?

_____

_____

_____

Which decisions place you at high risk if you haven't validated your assumptions about them?

_____

_____

_____

How might these decisions unfold in the future if there is a major flaw in your assumptions or in the degree of risk you are taking?

_____

_____

_____

Mentally walk down the path and picture what will happen if the divorce process and your decision making maintain their current direction. What are the chances everything will go as you hope?

_____

_____

_____

Where are you likely to end up if you choose to proceed on your own? Will you be okay later if you discover a major mistake or oversight?

_____

_____

_____

2. Seek Expert Perspective

In which of the following areas do you need to seek expert perspective in order to make the best decisions?

Financial _____

Real Estate _____

Legal _____

Emotional _____

Parenting _____

Relationships _____

Communication _____

Where will you find these resources?

_____

_____

_____

3. Expand Your Capacity

The divorce process places you in roles that are unfamiliar, and in which you may not be equipped to make good decisions. The input of others can provide you with the tools you need to navigate these new roles and evaluate your assumptions.

Your role is changing, and there are some new roles you will be assuming. In which of these new roles do you feel least confident?

_____

_____

_____

In what areas do you need to draw on the experience of others to help you be successful?

_____

_____

_____

4. Align with Your Best Self

Although you may feel inclined to isolate yourself during divorce, it's important to make an effort to engage with individuals who can provide support and expertise during the divorce process.

It's okay to admit you don't have all the answers. Who do you know who might have some valuable insights to share with you?

_____

_____

_____

What people can help you get in touch with your best self?

_____

_____

_____

How can you graciously accept feedback and input on your decision and actions? Even from your spouse or ex-spouse?

_____

_____

_____

5. Your Next Step

What small step can you take to move forward and seek support from others, in addition to your attorney?

_____

_____

_____

On a scale of 1-10, how important is this step to you? _____

What will be accomplished when you take this step?

_____

_____

_____

By when will you take this step?

_____

_____

_____

Whom will you ask for support?

_____

_____

_____

How Can a Personal Divorce Coach Help?

A personal Divorce Coach...

- explores with you key areas of decision making during the divorce process.
- ensures you're able to bring your best self forward to maintain clear and confident communication.
- helps you identify and understand the roles of other professionals—in addition to your attorney—who can provide assistance.
- makes referrals to those resources.
- works with you to clarify your purpose and remain true to your values, rendering decision making less difficult.

"To accept good advice is but to increase one's own ability"

— Johann Wolfgang von Goethe

Chapter 4

MISTAKE FOUR:
THROWING IN THE TOWEL

This divorce has dragged on for far longer than I ever thought it would, and it's taking a toll on me. I'm exhausted. I have no energy. I can't deal with this anymore. I just want to live in peace and not deal with the misery any longer. The money and the house don't matter at this point. All I want is to get away from all of this—and at this point I'm willing to do that at all costs.

The divorce process creates an overwhelming variety of negative emotions—shame, guilt, anger, betrayal, failure—that can wreak havoc on your mental and physical health. You're in a constant state of turmoil, and stress inevitably takes its toll. You feel ground down by the conflict, or the stony silence. You're exhausted and on the verge of just giving in to your spouse.

You feel as if you're drowning in a sea of never-ending rounds of surprise meetings, consultations, and mediations and you never know what's next. Your job performance and your relationship with your children are suffering, and it seems there just aren't enough hours in the day to do everything you need to do. The deck seems stacked against you, and the whole divorce process is completely unfair. You've become so worn down and tired of the whole mess that you're tempted to throw in the towel and move on with your life.

Consequences of Throwing in the Towel

Throwing in the towel may mean you end up settling for less than you deserve or paying out more than you can afford. It's rarely wise to give in "just to get it over with."

In giving up just to get it all over with, you may be temporarily easing stress (caused by negotiations and issues arising from the current divorce proceedings), but you may be creating more problems than you're solving. Instead of ironing out all the important issues in the original agreement—such as housing, the family pets, the vehicles, and matters concerning the children's religion, education and support—you may overlook critical details that keep you stuck in negotiation limbo forever. As a result, you may have years of meetings, consultations, negotiations, paperwork, and court proceedings ahead of you—and, of course, years of anger, shame, guilt, and anxiety. Throwing in the towel may bring you short-term relief, but you're risking your long-term wellbeing.

Insights from Personal Divorce Coaches

1. Shift your view from the past or present to a future vantage point to gain clarity, confidence, and courage.
2. Develop healthy coping mechanisms to help you through the temporary negative emotions you are having.
3. You may not have been through a divorce before, but you've been in stressful situations—and developed resilience. Think about how you coped.
4. Take the necessary time to clarify what is best for you and your family.

The Key Idea:

Draw on your past strengths and past accomplishments; develop your resilience to continue negotiating for what's most important to you.

Develop Clarity and Take Action

 ### 1. Walk down the Path

Take some time to examine the impact of just walking away and accepting the current terms.

Imagine it's five years from now. During your divorce, you threw in the towel and accepted the terms that were on the table. What's your life like now, based on those terms? (Paint a picture of your everyday life including where you are living, what you do each day, etc.)

_____

_____

_____

_____

_____

How do the decisions you are making right now impact that vision?

_____

_____

How do these decisions create more obstacles to overcome in the future?

_____

_____

_____

2. Seek Expert Perspective

The point of view and expertise of professionals can help to keep you from throwing in the towel. What expert perspective will help you in this situation?

_____

_____

_____

Where can you find that support?

_____

_____

_____

3. Expand Your Capacity

Answer the following questions about a past experience that required resilience:

When did you bounce back from a difficult time?

_____

_____

_____

How did you do it?

_____

_____

_____

What was your first small step?

_____

_____

_____

From whom did you get support?

_____

_____

_____

How did your resiliency impact others?

_____

_____

_____

4. Align with Your Best Self

For your family, friends and colleagues, you become a role model for "how to" or "how not to" handle yourself during tough times, especially in divorce.

Are you going to take the high road or the low road? How might you tell whether you are on the high road or the low road?

_____

_____

_____

In the future, how do you want to remember yourself and your ability to demonstrate resilience and overcome this very difficult time?

_____

_____

_____

How do you want to appear to others and what do you want them to learn from you about overcoming their own difficult situations?

_____

_____

_____

5. Your Next Step

What small step can you take to move forward, develop your resilience and continue negotiating for what's most important to you?

_____

_____

_____

On a scale of 1-10, how important is this step to you? _____

What will be accomplished when you take this step?

_____

_____

_____

By when will you take this step?

_____

_____

_____

Whom will you ask for support?

_____

_____

_____

How Can a Personal Divorce Coach Help?

A Personal Divorce Coach…

- helps you build energy reserves, coping skills, and resilience.
- works with you to look at the current offer and how your future will be impacted if you throw in the towel.
- examines different perspectives and scenarios with you.

"When you get into a tight place and everything goes against you, till it seems as though you could not hang on a minute longer, never give up then, for that is just the place and time that the tide will turn."

—Harriet Beecher Stowe

Chapter 5

MISTAKE FIVE: BETTING THE FARM ON ANOTHER RELATIONSHIP

I was completely blindsided with the divorce. I finally stopped feeling so sorry for myself and forced myself to get out and do some volunteer work. A month ago I met a man who's been showering me with attention; I'm spending more and more time with him. And now, he's told me he wants to spend the rest of his life with me! He says he really needs me!

Your divorce is not yet final, and you've met someone else. You both want to get married as soon as the divorce is complete, and you can't wait for the whole ordeal to be over so you can begin your new life. You're willing to do just about anything to speed up the process, including retracting some of your earlier requests and giving up some things you once thought were important to your future—like an agreement that awards you the house, a pension, and permanent alimony. You want to hurry up and settle this ugly divorce business before it scares away your new fiancé.

Consequences of Betting the Farm on Another Relationship

Wanting to bring an emotionally challenging and costly experience to a close as quickly and painlessly as possible is only natural, and this desire becomes even more pressing when you believe a new love and new life await you. During a divorce, you're in an extremely vulnerable state, and that sometimes leads to unwise decisions. Throwing caution to the wind, betting the farm on another relationship, and tossing away guarantees for future security is risky behavior.

Your focus should remain on ironing out the details of an equitable agreement with your spouse, no matter how long the negotiations take. Making choices driven by desperation or fear could be disastrous, and rushing your decision making in order to jump into another relationship can lead to huge regrets. It's important to tie up the details and put your past relationship to rest before you move on, and even more important that you proceed with caution. No matter how much in love you are, hasty decisions often cause huge regrets.

Insights from Personal Divorce Coaches

1. The presence of a new relationship has a significant impact on the desire to find a short-term solution, and your eagerness to make a quick decision could negatively affect the outcome of your divorce settlement.
2. Slow down the rush to leave this current situation. If the other person is committed to this new relationship, they will be there once the divorce settlement is completed.

The Key Idea:

End your current marriage well before counting on what a new relationship will provide.

Develop Clarity and Take Action

1. Walk down the Path

You're in love or involved in a new relationship and, as everyone knows, love is blind. Slow down and switch your focus to ending the current relationship using a sound decision-making approach.

If the new relationship were not a factor, what would you be asking for so that you can move ahead and transition to your new future?

_____

_____

_____

What would you want to retain (that you are now willing to give up) in the proposed settlement?

_____

_____

_____

Who or what might be affected by a hurried decision?

_____

_____

_____

2. Seek Expert Perspective

What do you need to know—and with whom can you consult—about your answers to the questions in "Walk down the Path"?

_____

_____

_____

Where will you find these resources?

_____

_____

_____

3. Expand Your Capacity

Just as a caterpillar becomes a butterfly, when a relationship ends, transformations occur that can signify new strength, new perspective, and new beginnings—and often an entirely new person emerges from the cocoon.

What have you learned about yourself through divorce that will help you to create a more fulfilling future?

_____

_____

_____

As you develop the new you, how do you picture your future?

_____

_____

_____

What do you need to learn or experience to help make that picture a reality?

_____

_____

_____

4. Align with Your Best Self

How does the decision you're making (about how you're ending your current relationship) align with your deepest values and your life purpose?

_____

_____

_____

Are there other relationships that may be impacted by this new love, like adult children, grandchildren, old friends? How do you balance the risk of losing precious relationships versus enjoying the new found pleasure of being adored?

_____

_____

_____

5. Your Next Step

What small step can you take to move forward to end your current relationship and finalize your divorce before moving on to a new relationship?

_____

_____

_____

On a scale of 1-10, how important is this step to you? _____

What will be accomplished when you take this step?

_____

_____

_____

By when will you take this step?

_____

_____

_____

Whom will you ask for support?

_____

_____

_____

How Can a Personal Divorce Coach Help?

A Personal Divorce Coach...

- walks with you down different paths (beginning a new relationship before ending the old, remarrying immediately, making desperate choices, etc.) to help you understand the potential risks and rewards of each option.
- helps you understand if and how your decisions align with your deepest values and life purpose.

> *"Never give up. And most importantly, be true to yourself.*
> *Write from your heart, in your own voice,*
> *and about what you believe in."*
>
> —Louise Brown

Chapter 6

MISTAKE SIX: WANTING GUARANTEES AND CERTAINTY

I'm scared and confused. This is more overwhelming than I ever thought it would be. I'm getting everything I asked for, but I don't know if it's good enough. Nothing seems to be written in stone; everything keeps changing. I don't know if I can go through this, not knowing for sure what is going to happen.

The whole divorce process is filled with uncertainties, regardless of who initiates the action, and feeling secure about your present and future is important, no matter what. Fear of the future is a normal reaction. We all have a basic need to enjoy a degree of certainty in our lives, and when that need isn't met, we feel threatened—and unable to make decisions.

Like many who go through divorce, you feel as if the rug is being pulled out from underneath you; so to cushion yourself from the blow, you try to nail down every detail. But instructing your lawyer to pursue less consequential items, like the TV or stereo system, means you may be spending more money than the items are worth.

You are bewildered and uncertain about the whole settlement, and you're worried if you're making a deal that's right for you and your future. Although your spouse is offering everything you asked for, you have no idea if that's enough. You don't know if you'll always have a job, or be able to afford a house, or have enough for retirement. So you just can't make a decision.

Consequences of Wanting Guarantees and Certainty

If you fail to act within a reasonable amount of time, the offer you're considering may be unfavorably changed or withdrawn. Although you worry about doing the right thing, if you hesitate too long, "analysis paralysis" may frustrate your spouse and ultimately result in the retraction of a generous offer.

When one party stalls, lawyers sometimes step in and try to force a settlement using strong-arm tactics. As negotiations crumble, you may either lose ground or face going to court for legal adjudication.

Insights from Personal Divorce Coaches

1. Use experts in their fields (financial planners, for example) to help you understand the ramifications of the settlement terms.
2. Look at each element and determine how it fits into your ideal future.
3. Explore alternative scenarios, including potential best-case and worst-case situations. Walk down the pathway and envision how they might play out in the future.
4. Readjust your approach and attitude when negotiating with your spouse. When you put up resistance, have unrealistic expectations, or are overcome by fear of the future, you are hindering your efforts to acquire needed assets and effect an agreement.
5. Work to shift your need to resist your spouse's offer.
6. Beware of having unrealistic expectations about the legal process. Become knowledgeable about your finances: Know how much you need to survive, how much will afford you a reasonable quality of life, and what amount you need to thrive.

> ## The Key Idea:
> Slow down. Take time to
> understand the settlement terms
> and identify any generous provisions
> that may be present.

Develop Clarity and Take Action

1. Walk down the Path

Initially, you may experience fear and hesitancy. Try to look down the road beyond these concerns.

How do the options presented in the proposed agreement support your desired future?

_____

_____

_____

If these options don't support your desired future, what needs to be changed?

_____

_____

_____

2. Seek Expert Perspective

What information are you lacking right now that would help you better understand the settlement terms?

_____

_____

_____

Where can you get this information?

_____

_____

_____

3. Expand Your Capacity

Avoid seeing crises as insurmountable problems. You can't change the fact that highly stressful events happen, but you can change how you interpret and respond to these events. Accept that change is a part of living. Focus on the circumstances you can influence or control rather than those you feel you have no control over.

What can you see beyond the present that points to how future circumstances may be a little better?

_____

_____

_____

What circumstances can you focus on over which you have control or influence?

_____

_____

_____

What responses to circumstances can you control or influence?

_____

_____

_____

What resources do you need to exercise that control?

_____

_____

_____

4. Align with Your Best Self

When one door closes, another opens—and you want to be sure you're ready to take the next big step with confidence, clarity, and courage.

Besides clarity, confidence, and courage, what other qualities do you need to develop to facilitate your next big step?

_____

_____

_____

What success have you had in the past that brought out the best in you?

_____

_____

_____

Thinking back on that success, how can you adjust your thinking and emotions to achieve a positive outcome and overcome your fears?

_____

_____

_____

5. Your Next Step

What small step can you take to slow down, understand the settlement terms, and feel more comfortable with your future?

_____

_____

_____

On a scale of 1-10, how important is this step to you? _____

What will be accomplished when you take this step?

_____

_____

_____

By when will you take this step?

_____

_____

_____

Whom will you ask for support?

_____

_____

_____

How Can a Personal Divorce Coach Help?

A personal Divorce Coach…

- helps you determine what level of certainty you need to be comfortable.
- puts you in touch with other experts who can assist with your specific needs (i.e. financial professionals).
- works with you to alleviate the fear that is keeping you from making decisions.
- helps you build resiliency.

"Faith means living with uncertainty, feeling your way through life, letting your heart guide you like a lantern in the dark."

—Dan Millman

Chapter 7

HOW TO HIRE A PERSONAL
DIVORCE COACH

Turning to a personal Divorce Coach, an experienced, nonjudg-mental professional, can help you as you examine your feelings and clarify your choices. A personal Divorce Coach encourages you to look at the entire picture and provides support as you evaluate your readiness for change. A personal Divorce Coach helps you become better prepared and consider every aspect of each decision you must make. Here are some guidelines to consider as you think about hiring a personal Divorce Coach:

Hire a personal Divorce Coach as early as possible in the process.

To avoid costly emotional and financial mistakes during the divorce process, hire a personal Divorce Coach as early as possible. Many of the most important decisions, especially those that impact finances and relationships, are made at the beginning of the divorce process, and having a personal Divorce Coach by your side during those early days can be beneficial. Personal Divorce Coaches will help you explore your options, organize your thoughts, gather materials, and make informed decisions. In addition to supporting you in each stage, they also save you time and money.

Take advantage of the initial exploratory session offered by personal Divorce Coaches.

You need to feel comfortable with the particular personal Divorce Coach you hire. The best way to get a sense of how you'll relate to a particular coach is to schedule an exploratory session, which can be in person or over the telephone. (Personal Divorce Coaching is often done via telephone. Remember, personal Divorce Coaching is not limited by geography because personal Divorce Coaches do not give legal advice.)

The exploratory session will help you clarify in your own mind what you want to accomplish and how coaching can support you through the rough spots or help you overcome hurdles. And it provides an opportunity for you to ask questions or express any of your concerns. You take something of value from the session whether or not you choose this person as your coach, because it will help illuminate where you are and what obstacles you may encounter.

Inquire about the personal Divorce Coach's specific training and experience.

Personal Divorce Coaching covers domains not ordinarily part of any other life coaching. The enormity of change, the intensity of emotions and engagement in the legal process create unique challenges for someone who has not been trained in how to most effectively work with you in these circumstances. Divorce has the capacity to overwhelm everything, so you want a coach with a good bag of tools to help you through the process.

In addition to training, a personal Divorce Coach brings people and resources representing a wide variety of professionals and providers, which may be valuable to you at various stages in the divorce process.

Inquire about the personal Divorce Coach's ethics and professional responsibilities.

Personal Divorce Coaches operate among many other professionals who are licensed to serve the public. Professional ethics and commitment to responsibilities are the hallmark of any professional, and a well-respected professional is generally an individual who maintains high ethical standards and makes every effort to fulfill responsibilities. You will be best served by someone who clearly outlines their professional ethics and responsibilities to you.

Ask all your questions—even the tough ones.

Divorce can be an all-consuming process, and you need to have confidence that the coach you choose can help you through the rough spots in a manner that meets your expectations—so don't be afraid to ask tough questions. It is best to find out if your coach is a good fit as early in the relationship as possible. If there is a deal breaker for you, it's best to throw that on the table and address the issue right away. Usually, the way in which someone answers a tough question is what lets you know if they are the professional you want to work with.

Express your needs and expectations.

Only you know what your needs and expectations are, and you shouldn't hesitate to express these openly to your coach. Remember, your personal Divorce Coach will work with your best interests in mind, so the more you communicate, the better you and your coach can work together to evaluate, adjust and learn. For this reason alone, you should find a coach who puts you at ease.

Hire a personal Divorce Coach who has experience coaching all stages of divorce.

Each stage of divorce has a different focus, and thus requires a specific awareness of and approach to client needs: Coaching during the legal process of divorce is not the same as coaching during the pre-divorce or post-divorce stages. People have different responses and needs during these transitions, and they often become frustrated. A personal Divorce Coach is an understanding guide who can provide the sustenance you need for your entire journey.

Don't assume that only a coach of the same gender is best for you.

Gender may not even be a factor, so why eliminate a coach based on that sole criterion? Choosing a personal Divorce Coach of the opposite gender may be advantageous because you'll have access to a different perspective and can explore your actions and conversations through someone else's vantage point. One benefit of engaging a coach is you're afforded the opportunity to stretch—and choosing a coach of the opposite gender is an automatic stretch! At least try it out in an initial exploratory session.

Hiring a personal Divorce Coach is an important step in the divorce process. Choose a personal Divorce Coach who is willing to make the entire journey with you—from pre-divorce to post-divorce—a guide and advisor who will provide you with all the tools you need, including reality checks, exploring options, and helping you communicate more effectively.

The personal Divorce Coach ensures you have a person at your side who's completely in your court, a person who will help you handle the thousands of details and issues you face in the most effective and beneficial way possible. At the same time, you'll gain an expert in your corner who'll help you become focused, confident, and self-reliant.

RESOURCES

Books

Deal With It! How To Manage The Conflict In Your Life
    Eudine Herbert, M.ED., NPCM, CDC® 2010.
    Ten practical lessons for dealing with conflict.

Decisive. How to Make Better Choices In Life And Work.
    Chip Heath and Dan Heath. 2013.
    A simple approach to recognizing the pitfalls in decision making and how to ensure you make better decisions.

Dignity, The Essential Role It Plays in Resolving Conflict
    Donna Hicks, PhD. 2011.
    The author has defined in such a profound way the impact that loss of dignity can have on everyone and how restoring dignity can bring us together.

Divorce and New Beginnings
    Genevieve Clapp, Ph.D. 2000.
    Especially good for helping you develop a roadmap for all of those tricky parenting issues during and after divorce.

Divorce and Recovery: 101 Stories about Surviving and Thriving after Divorce
    Jack Canfield, Mark Victor Hansen, Patty Hansen. 2008.
    Inspiring short stories to help you realize you are not alone.

Mars and Venus Starting Over: A Practical Guide to Finding Love Again After a Painful Breakup, Divorce, or Loss of a Loved One
John Gray, Ph.D. 2002.
Especially helpful in identifying how to use the emotions we most resist to heal, let go, and be ready to move on to a new future.

Oasis in the Overwhelm: 60–second strategies for balance in a busy world
Millie Grenough. 2005.
Four simple strategies to strengthen the four domains of your total health.

Splitting: Protecting Yourself While Divorcing Someone with Borderline or Narcissistic Personality Order
Bill Eddy, LCSW, JD. and Randi Kreger. 2011.
A perspective for those who are dealing with someone who seems to come from an alternate reality.

The Good Karma Divorce: Avoid Litigation, Turn Negative Emotions into Positive Actions and Get on with the Rest of Your Life
Judge Michele Lowrance. 2010
A judge's perspective on how to take the negative emotions of divorce and change them into positive actions to help you move on with your life.

The Journey from Fear To Love: Waking Up and Walking the "Evolutionary Relationship" Path With Your Partner.
Laurie Cameron. 2008.
Learn to respond to your partner with love instead of being blocked by fears. Available only through www.wakeupenterprises.com.

Thriving After Divorce
Tonja Evetts Weimer. 2010.
A guide to help you use your divorce as an inspiration for positive change.

Transcending Divorce: 10 Essential Touchstones for Finding Hope and Healing in Your Heart
>   Alan Wolfelt, PhD. 2008.
>   Dealing with love and loss and the divorce transition process.

True Purpose
>   Tim Kelley. 2009.
>   If you want to seek input from your high self or universal spirit, Tim Kelly lays out a process for connecting to what he refers to as your "Trusted Advisors."

You Can Heal Your Life
>   Louse L. Hay. 1984
>   This book is packed with wisdom about how you can harness your own power to change your life.

Online Resources

Articles by Mark Baer from Huffington Post
www.huffingtonpost.com/mark-baer

Attorney Mark Baer is recognized as a thought leader in many areas of Family Law for his provocative and forward-thinking ideas on improving the way in which Family Law is handled.

For more information about how to develop resilience, go to the APA website: www.apa.org/helpcenter/road-resilience.aspx

For professionals facing high conflict cases or issues:
www.highconflictinstitute.com

For information on becoming a CDC Certified Divorce Coach®:
www.certifieddivorcecoach.com

Finding a CDC Certified Divorce Coach®:
www.certifieddivorcecoach.com/find-a-divorce-coach

PRAISE FOR

PERSONAL
DIVORCE COACHING

"From my first phone session I felt empowered: I came away with a sense of direction, realistic goals, and an action plan. Most importantly, I had renewed self-esteem. Working with a personal Divorce Coach helped me acknowledge my priorities—and a way to achieve them."

—Rosana, Sydney Australia
Coach: Carolyn Madden
CDC Certified Divorce Coach®
www.DivorceCoachingAustralia.com.au

"Cheryl's coaching made all the difference for my husband and me: She was a neutral advocate for us both and helped us see a clear picture of the best possible outcome. The arguing stopped and was replaced with cooperation. Working with Cheryl set the tone for the future and has made a lasting impact on the relationship we now have."

—J.S., Irvine, CA
Coach: Cheryl Nielsen
CDC Certified Divorce Coach®
Author of *Meritage Divorce*
www.MeritageDivorce.com

"Using a personal Divorce Coach enabled me to find the best legal representation to protect myself and my daughter through a complicated custody and visitation battle. I was never comfortable with my first attorney, but I didn't know what to do. Working with Debra, I was able to quickly switch lawyers; I shudder to think what would have happened if I had remained with my initial lawyer."

—Leslie, Massachusetts
Coach: Debra Block
CDC Certified Divorce Coach®, MBA
www.DebraBlockDivorceCoach.com

"After over a decade of on-again, off-again attempts to improve my 24-year-old marriage, I found myself in a familiar and unhappy spot. I resolved this time it would be different, so I reached out to a personal Divorce Coach. Debra provides a fresh, knowledgeable perspective to some challenging issues, and affords me access to her professional network. By utilizing a personal Divorce Coach, I don't have to navigate the treacherous waters alone."

—T.R., Massachusetts
Coach: Debra Block
CDC Certified Divorce Coach®, MBA
www.DebraBlockDivorceCoach.com

"My husband was making my life miserable. I just wanted the whole thing over and was even willing to throw in the towel. Without coaching I would not have the strength or endurance to press on. Coaching has provided me the encouragement and guidance to stay the course, to work with my attorney, and not give up."

—M.G., Massachusetts
Coach: Debra Block
CDC Certified Divorce Coach®, MBA
www.DebraBlockDivorceCoach.com

"I knew I wanted a divorce, but after two years of separation, I still couldn't bring myself to finalize the paperwork. I believe if I had not had Merry as my coach these past four months, I never would have moved forward. I would have continued going in circles with my thoughts, doing nothing. Merry is my sounding board and confidante. I feel safe and respected with her; she has no agenda other than to help me discover what I want, and determine how to language my requests to my attorney. My divorce is now final, but I'm not letting go of Merry quite yet. I continue to work with her to help me design my new life."

—C.C., Alberta, Canada
Coach: Merry Berger
CDC Certified Divorce Coach©
www.certifieddivorcecoach.com/merryberger

"Working with Elaine helped me recognise that focusing on the past was holding me back, and that I wasn't taking responsibility for myself. I was blaming my ex for everything. Working with Elaine was like unlocking the door to my future. "

—Nicky, New Plymouth, New Zealand
Coach: Elaine Taylor
CDC Certified Divorce Coach©
www.lifelift.co.nz

CONNECT WITH THE AUTHORS

Pegotty and Randall Cooper can be reached through their website:
www.certifieddivorcecoach.com/contact-us

Printed in Great Britain
by Amazon

66945550R00047